For Thea

This is a second edition.
First published in 2016 by Nobrow Ltd.
27 Westgate Street, London E8 3RL

Published in the US by Nobrow (US) Inc.
Printed in Latvia on FSC assured paper.

ISBN: 978-1-910620-03-8
Order from www.nobrow.net

ALEXIS DEACON

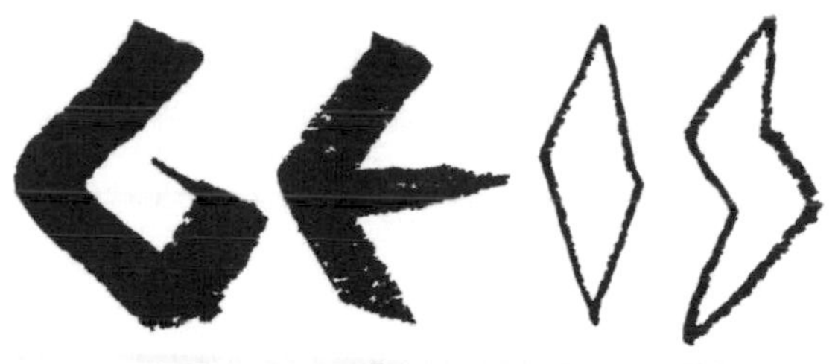

A MATTER OF LIFE & DEATH

NOBROW

London - New York

geis / ˈgɛʃ /

Geis, pronounced *gesh*, is a Gaelic word for a taboo or curse. When a geis is placed upon you, it is like a spell that cannot be broken and certain rules must be obeyed. You might be prohibited from calling upon the aid of wolves, for example, or from breaking into someone's kitchen. If you ignore or break a geis, the consequences are dire.

But a geis is always broken.

As soon as it is spoken or written,
your fate is set.

The great chief Matarka knew
that death was near at hand.

Having named no heir,
she made her Will.
There would be a contest.
Fate would choose the one
fit to take her place.

The rich, the strong,
the wise, the powerful,
many gave their names
in hope of being chosen.

But when the night came...

...fifty souls alone were summoned.
Why am I here?

Dragged out of bed in the middle of the night–
No warning, no apology–
And I was having such peaceful dreams too–
What is this?
Your honour, you do surprise me!
This is the Last Will and Testament of our chief.
Only the undersigned may contest.
So Matarka is dead at last.
Gods rest her soul but she might have waited...
...until morning.
Take this and sign.
What is it?
Just sign, will you! People are waiting.
Take and sign.
GODS!
Do we sit and gaze at this corpse all night?
Who commands here?
When do we begin this so-called contest?

Brother, if you will excuse me, might I be permitted to speak?

I have not been long at court but already I know who the great people are.

I see you all in this hall:

the Chief Judge,

the High Priestess,

the Lord Chamberlain,

the Grand Wizard.

While Matarka lived, she ruled...
...but Matarka is dead.
Do you still follow her will?

I say you hold the power in your own hands.
You should name your own chief.

I command the army. I should be chief!

Never!
No!!

gurgle...

Gods protect us!
Matarka is not dead!

But I touched her hand. I felt no pulse. It's not possible!

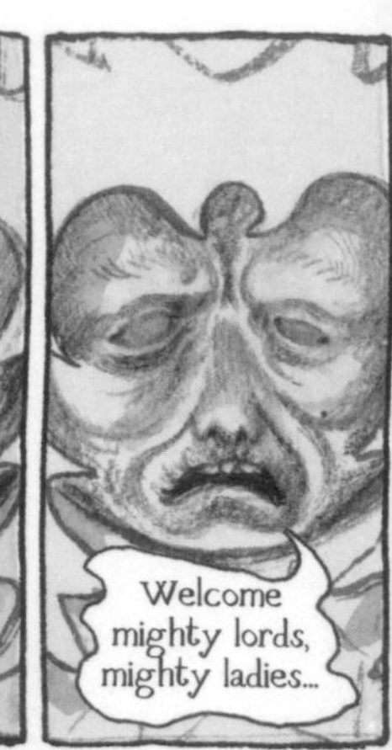
Welcome mighty lords, mighty ladies...

The time of your trial has come.

I am Niope, the sorceress.

Prepare yourselves...

...for I have come to test you.

Magic!

Let the first test begin!

A good chief should know the land.
All the land.

Like seed on the wind I scatter you.

Find your way back to me...
...before the light of the next dawn touches the castle door...

...or no chief will you be!

AAAAAAAAAA

WOOOOAH!

WAAAAAAA!

OOOOGO
ARRR!

SCRAFF!

SHOOF!

SPLASH!

shlok.

?

Where am I?

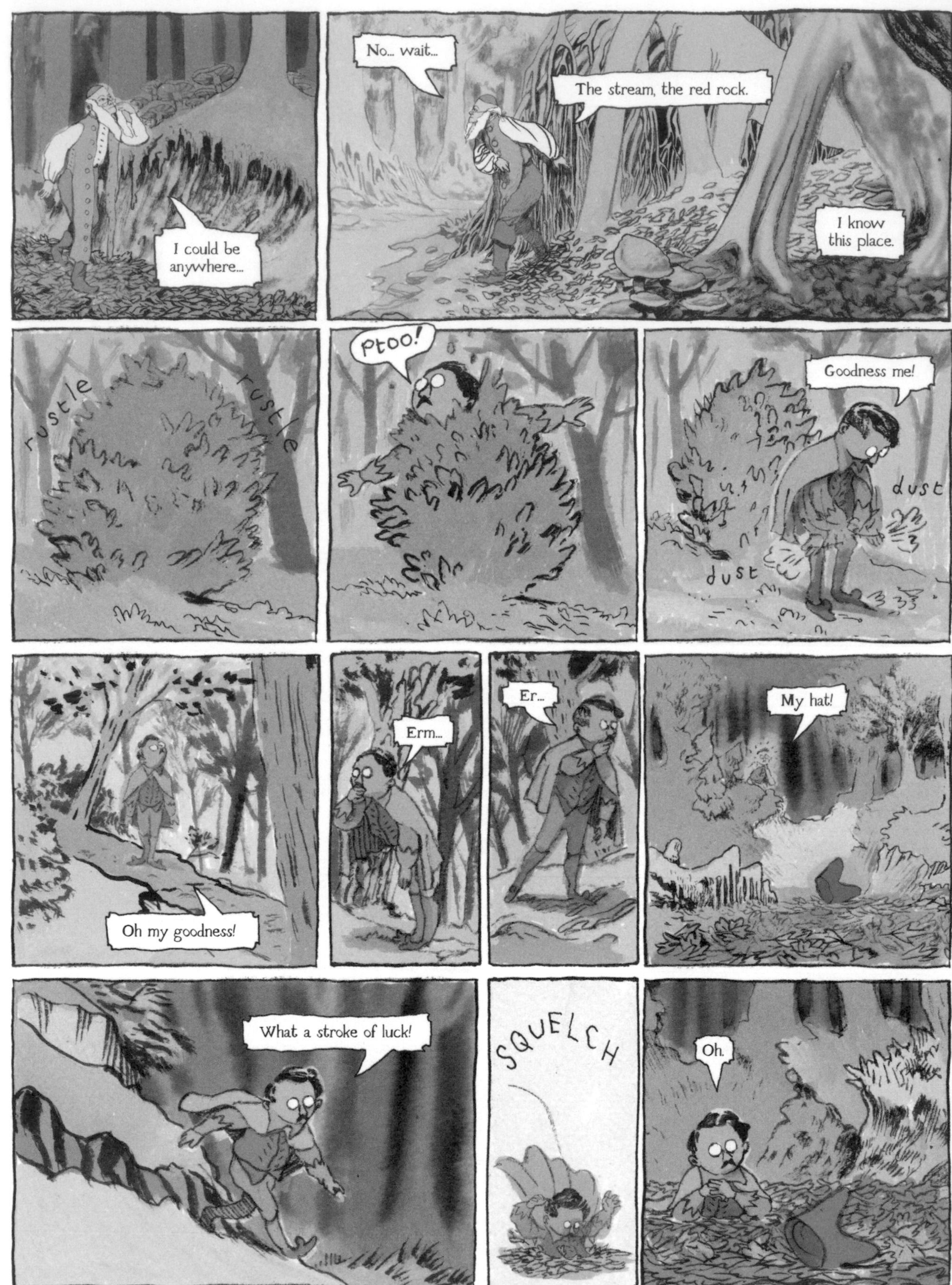
I could be anywhere...
No... wait...
The stream, the red rock.
I know this place.
rustle rustle
Ptoo!
Goodness me!
dust
dust
Oh my goodness!
Erm...
Er...
My hat!
What a stroke of luck!
SQUELCH
Oh.

CRACK

What's that?
CRASH

TINKLE
There's someone downstairs!

Ben?!

I can explain.

It seems a lifetime of study has not been wasted!

I know where I am.

This is the heart of the Black Forest.

Who is this sorceress?

By what right does she fling us around like toys?

Gods, what a monster!
This is no game!

Are we all facing dangers like this?

Now what is one supposed to do in this situation, I forget?
Was it move...
Or not move?

HELP!

Ah...

Not move.

Well, I had a nice life, I suppose.

Can't say I expected to go this way.

No regrets though.

Except, I wonder...

...if I had asked Anita...

Artur, is that you?
...

It's Nelson. Whatever you do, don't move!

ROOOAAR!

Phew!

I made it.

Was that merely luck...

...or was it something more?

hm.

!

ouch.

Hello?

Servants?

Citizens?

Anyone?

Oh dear.

AAAA
IEE

mphfl!
GASP!
How did this happen? I didn't enter my name.
My parents must have done it.
They must have bought me a place.
Are they trying to get rid of me?
Well, I am your daughter, do you hear!
Nothing can change that.

Sigh.
I'm no chief. I'll go back to the sorceress and withdraw from the contest.
ugh...
Magic.
Strong magic.
Death magic.
O, my chief, what have you done?
SCREEEEEEEE

Ha ha!
I must be the first to return!
What will Toras and Caliphas say when I come back before them?
This is my chance.
I'll show them.
I can win this contest.

I will be the one.

Hello?
Is anyone there?

Am I the first?
Have you seen my brothers?

Congratulations, Councillor Nemas.

You have passed my test.

I am the first to return.

That is no small feat.

You are not the first.

The Kite Lord's daughter? What is she doing here?

She is no great person. Pay her no mind.

Erm...
What's wrong with you?

Io's reward for returning first was to learn the truth.

The truth? What truth?

There will be but one chief, no challenger, no rival.

Well... Yes...
That's why we are being tested.

She means only one of us will survive the contest.

WHAT?

Only the strongest can live. That is the world's true nature.

That's madness! I withdraw!

She won't allow us.

Bah! She has no power over me!
GUARDS!
GUARDS!

Wha...!

HEY!

You're wrong. We gave ourselves to her.

oof.
I did no such thing.

The paper we signed.
That was Matarka's Will. I read it several times.

Look again, fool.
I will lift the veil from your eyes...

GEIS!

What is it?

What have I done?

Matarka's Will was enchanted.

It is the Geis, the binding fate.
Written in the blood of your chief; paid for with the last of her life.

Now I am bound to find the true chief among you.
None who sign may refuse this trial.
Show me where it is written that we must die in the process!

It is not written.
With the power I am given, I will take your lives.

For the rest, I claim you all! Your hearts will beat to feed my magic; your bodies will be shells for my puppets and my slaves; your minds will be shattered and broken.

Eek!
What have you done to him?

He died in my power. I made him my slave.
The same fate awaits all of you.

All but one, that is.

Why don't you just kill us now and have done with it?

I cannot. The Geis binds us all alike.
You are bound to be tried and I am bound to test you. This bond cannot be broken.

What about people who don't come back in time? Or people who give up the test?

Them, I will kill.
RARR

Others are arriving.
The time for talk is ended.

We shall play a game,
we three.

Not one word may you
speak of what you know.

It will be our secret.

Welcome, Lady Judge.

You have passed my first test.

What is
happening here?

Ha ha ha ha ha ha
ha ha ha ha ha ha!

Well, I am rather damp but my hat, at least, has survived unscathed.
squelch squelch squelch squelch

Thank you again for saving me, by the way.
Oh...

I didn–
I thought my number was up!

It was so clear!
Everything came into focus.

It's funny how that happens at such times.
Now I will call on Anita the first chance I get!
squelch squelch

What would she think...
...if I was made chief?

Hmph!
squelch

What if she made you chief, Nelson?
The sorceress, I mean.

Hmmm...
You can't bring back the dead...
...and you can't make someone love you.

I believe I would rebuil–
HEY! LOOK! It's Ben and Eloise!

Cobalt's Wood!
Some hideous cave!
Somebody's kitchen!
Sinking mud!

I am just thankful we are all alive!
You can say that again.

My friends, I am very much afraid.
Er... You are?

Afraid of what, Eloise?
Of this sorceress. Of her magic.

It took great power to make that spell.
Great power.

Power like that...

...comes at a cost.

You're telling me. Look at my trousers!
Oh my!
What are you saying?
It is called Death Magic.

Without fuel there is no fire... Artur, give me your hat.

My hat?
Erm...

BEHOLD!
Er...

Death magic.
Ah.

Are we to be cooped up here all day and all night?

Of course not, Judge. You are not my prisoners.

The terms of the test are merely that you return before dawn.

Then we are free to go?

When the first light of the morning sun touches the castle doors, they will be sealed and the second test will begin.

What you do before that time you do of your own free will. Perhaps you should consider getting some rest?

One word of caution.

If you are not within when the doors are sealed...

...you will fail and your contest will be ended.

That being said...

...you are free to go.

Excuse us, m'lady!

NEMAS!

We've got to warn...

...
!?

The spell!
Ack!
Ack!
You are hurt.

This is it. From now on...

...it is my life...

...or death.

NEMAS!

What are you doing? Stop!

Don't you understand?

I have no choice.

I must be strong.

You think I'm weak?

You know nothing about me.

I can be strong.

Is that better?

Forgive me!

There is no other way. We must accept it. This is our fate.

Do it quickly.

Tell me what the sorceress told us!

What?

Tell me what the sorceress told us.
Tell me the secret.

But you know... she told us that...

...that...

hu...

Ack!
Ack!
Ack!

Ack!
Ack!
Ack!

TAM!

Mistress?
Saddle Ragdoll and Marble.
Meet me at the front gate in half an hour...
...and come armed.

?
Councillor, are you unwell?
What time is it?
Erm...
About ten in the evening, I think...
...but...
?
To Mertan the armourer, and quickly!

Eloise, I've been thinking about what you said.

And, do you know, I'm not sure I want to do battle with a Death sorceress.
I think I'd rather go to bed.
What a good idea.

Ben, you have your family to think of.
Yes, my poor Agnes!

Go back to your homes, my friends. You're right. This fight is not for you.

But Eloise, we'll not leave you to face this woman alone!
I'm afraid you must. There is nothing you can do.

Farewell, all of you!
Eloise!

Eloise...

GOOD LUCK!

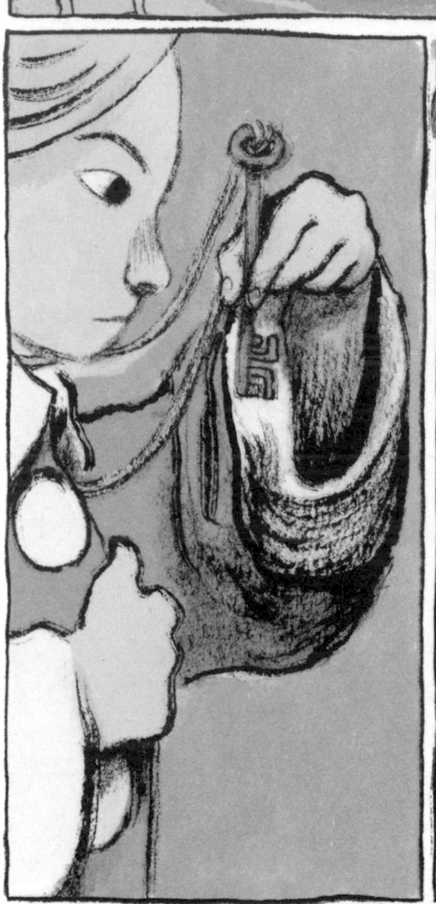

CRREAK!

Osha.
Z

Z

Osha.
Z

Osha!

OSHA!
SAVE US!

Are you alright?
Oh, mistress it's you!
I thought the angels had come for me!

Osha, I think I'm in trouble. Does Father have any books on the old magic?

Child, your father has books about everything.

YAR!

YAR!

YAR!

woah!

Hey! Where's my fare?

There are twelve pieces of silver here. You can have as much again if you'll give me the use of your carriage for the night.

There are one or two things I must do...
...before the sun rises.

Well, gentlemen, once again we come to a parting of the ways.
I hope we did the right thing letting Eloise go off alone.
Really, she gave us no choice in the matter.

I don't know...
I begin to think I should have gone with her.

Do what you must. For my part, I am going home to my family.
Goodnight, Ben!

Well, what do you think?
Surely, Eloise was right. What could we do?

I am rather sad I'll never be chief though.

Goodnight, Nelson. Thank you again for saving my life.
Goodnight, Artur, old friend.

It's getting late. I'll stop here at the Crossroads Inn. Join me, if you'd care to?

Perhaps they are right...

What difference could I make?

One builds, the other tears down. They are opposites... but perhaps there could not be one without the other. Without life, death has no meaning. That is sure. Who is to say what life would be without death?

I've heard it said that of the two, Life Magic is stronger. But life has never threatened to conquer all death...

Can I bring you anything else, sir?

Sir?

Oh. Hm?
Can I bring you anything else?

Oh, no, thank you, miss... I think I shall just go to bed.
I am very tired.

Very well, sir. Please follow me. I will show you to your room.

Please snuff out the candle when you go to sleep.
Of course.
Thank you, miss.

Now let me see... magic... magic... magic...

We have several, mostly histories of dubious provenance... but wait...

Yes, I thought so!

What is it, Osha?

It is a book, a very old book, older even than Osha. Hee hee hee.

Some of the text here is in a script I cannot read.

Put your lamp on the table, my dear.

This is not one of your father's books.

It has been in the family for generations.
Look.

SCREAM!
SAVE US!

WORM!

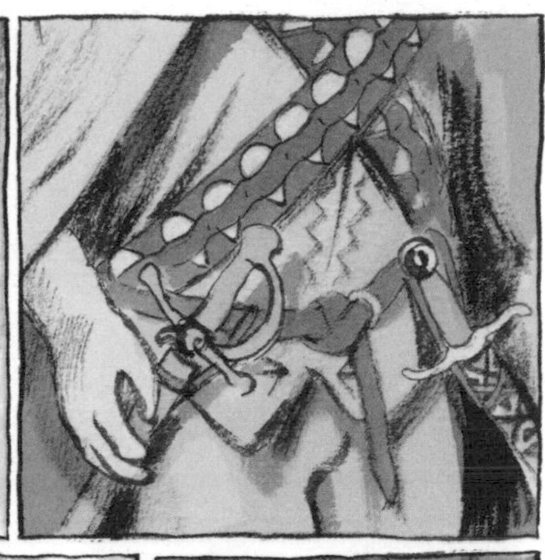

tok
tok

ta-tak
ta-tak

tok
tok
tok

Enter.

Why if it isn't the General's little brother. You are lucky to find us awake.

There is no rest for the wicked, so they say.

Very true, no doubt.
And how may the wicked serve you at so late an hour?

I need poison for blade and cup, both the quick and the slow.

Let us see what we can do.

Z
Anita?
Fair one, are you there?
help me! I'm dying!
Eek!
I can't help you! I can't help you!
help!
help!
help!
help.
help.
help!
help.
help!
help.
help.
help.
help!
ANITA!

I am here, Artur.
I love you. My love for you can never die.
BEHOLD!
DEATH MAGIC!
AH!
Anita?
Anita?
ANITA
DEATH
Anita
DEATH
HELP!

Help me! Someone! Please!
Help!
Oh, look, it is Artur. He is dying.
How sad.
htlph
Well, I must be getting home now.
Good night, Artur.
hff
Yes... good night.

So...
You mean to challenge me?

Village witch.

You do not answer?

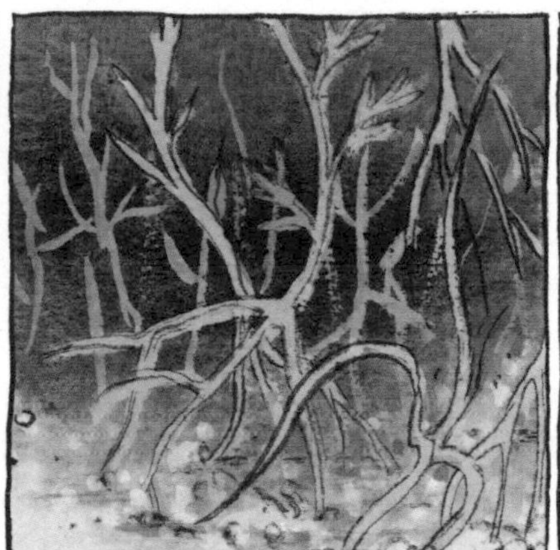

Let it be as you wish.

CRACK

?

ha ha ha ha ha

So you do know a little magic, then?

It will not be enough to save you.

?

!

choke!

...

Very good.

But your memory is as limited as your magic.
You have forgotten our first meeting.

I am not bound to my body.

ᛒᛟᛞᛁ ᛏᛟᚹᛗᚱ
I can take another.

Can you?

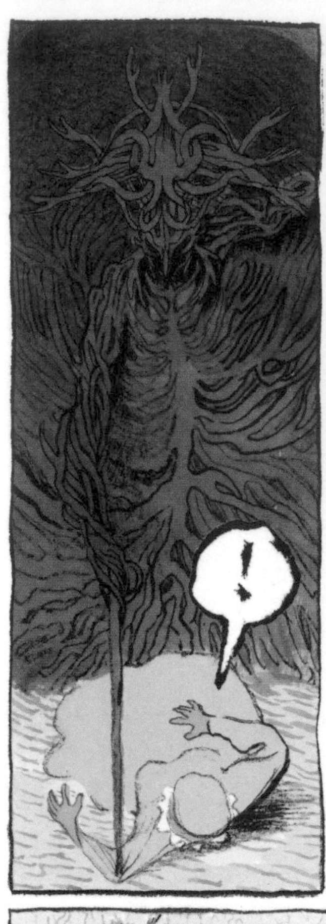
!

I won't kill you.

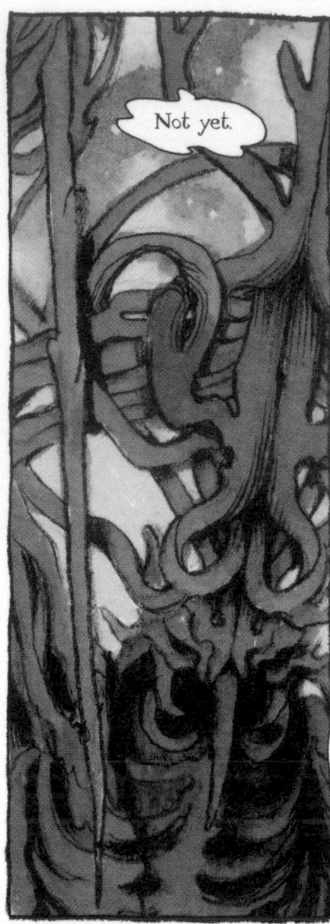
Not yet.

I am bound by a promise.

But who knows?

Perhaps, something else will do it for me?

I think we have had enough
of your magic.

?!

I do not kill you, Wizard.

Though I bring the wolf to water...

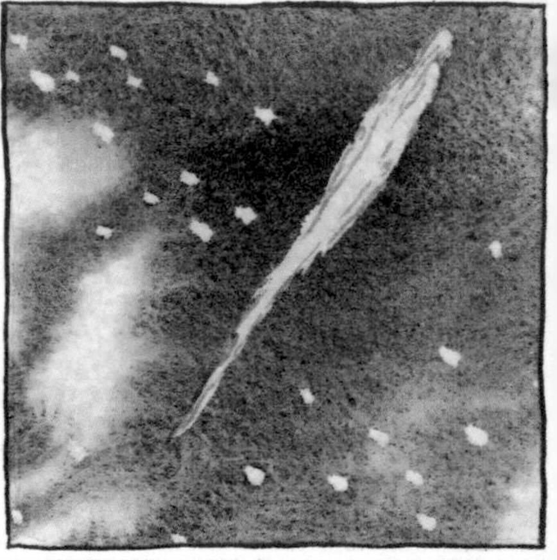

Eloise!
Eloise! I'm coming!
OW OW OW
OWOOOO!
BOOM!

Ah.
RARRR!
Ah.
Oh, Gods! How does this go again?
Prime the pan! Prime the pan!
Clear the pan.
Ready the shot.
Measure the charge.
Pour the charge.
Tamp it down. Tamp it down.
Ram the shot.
Present and...
RARRR

EEK!

TAM!
GET THE
BIG ONE!

Whup!
yelp!
OWOOO!
Wait!
Let them go! They won't hurt us. They are afraid.

Eloise...

Is she still alive?

There is a heartbeat but she is gravely wounded.

Artur, give me your cloak.

RRRRRIP!
Oh.

We must get her to my hospice.
NO!

She must go to the Capital.
The Capital, why?
Her situation is worse than you know.
She is curs–
Ack!
Ack!
Ack!
Mistress!
Mistress...
Ack!
We cannot delay. We must ride for my hospice at once.
URRR
RARRR
Dear Gods! That thing isn't dead!
We go to the Capital.
We go now.

Clink
jangle

Is someone there?

Good evening, everyone.

Daddy!

Ben.
Agnes, my love.

What of the contest?
You didn't win?

No, my love, I did not.

Then who is to be chief?
Not Judge Joyce, I hope?
Let's talk about it in the morning.
All I can think of is my bed and a nice hot drink.
Oh my! Just look at your trousers!
As for you, little ones, you should have been in bed long ago.
We were waiting for you, Daddy.
Well it is bedtime for one and all now.
That means you too, little miss.
My love?
Yes?
Is the contest really over? Have you lost for sure?
It's just... you would have made such a fine chief.
I have made my decision.

SCREAM!

The dawn!

Come on, Kite...
just a little farther.

AIEE!

WOAH!
!
The Kite! Keep her Steady!
ELOISE!
NO.
Oh, Gods!
I can't hold on! She's slipping!
GIRL! GIRL!
Give me the weight.
WHAT?
TRUST ME!
WOOOAH!
OH! HELP!
Climb up! Take control!
Oh, Gods!

What do I know about kites?
I took my father's advice.
I learned bookkeeping.
How many times have I nearly died today?
Not once has bookkeeping been any use whatsoever!
Stop.
Do not touch the sunlight.
It burns.
Get back to the raft as quickly as you can.
We are coming in to land.

Ben? What are you doing?
Won't you come back to bed?
GASP!
BEN!

HEY!
?

Beg pardon, sir, but are you in this here contest?

Er... yes... why?
Climb up and right quick.

I'm to get ye to the castle before dawn.
Erm...
But who are you?

Just climb up, will you?

Don't you know the expression?

Never look a gift horse in the mouth!

Brace yourselves!
Here...
...it...
...comes!

****!

Uuuuh...

Hello again.

I've thought about it.
I've thought about it a lot.

There is but one path open to us.
We either take it or we don't.

There is no other way.

Good grief!

What happened to your face?

CRACK!

Leave me alone, Nemas!
Curse you!

The sun is almost on the door! You'll kill us both!

I can't let you live...
Can I?
We two alone know the truth.

What are you talking about?
You won't trick me again!
Without you...

...I have a chance.

You mean to kill us all?
Is that it?

I think I might be the one. The true chief.

WHAT!?

I have to try.

I am going to try.

Is your life...

...worth so much more than ours?
WOOSH!

No...
CLANG

CLANG!
I don't know!

But I won't give it up...

...without...

...fighting.

I've killed her!

The slow poison.

I have killed her...

CLANG!
RRRR!

CLING!

CLANG!

CLANG!

MISTRESS!

...and it was all in vain.

Tam and you others,
help me get everyone inside!

Mistress, you're hurt...
It's nothing.

Quickly! Quickly!

Get them inside at once.

The things you wanted are all here...
Tam, you have to go. Take Ragdoll and Marble back home.

Thank you for all you have done.

Goodbye!

CLANG

The first test has now ended.
Let the second test begin.

Thanks to Isabel Greenberg, Viviane Schwarz, Becky Norris, Hannah Hayward and Frances and Alastair Currie for their help making this book.

BOOK TWO

A GAME WITHOUT RULES

Geis continues in Book Two, *A Game Without Rules*... COMING SOON.